SO-CPF-296

THE ESSENTIAL GUIDE
TO THE

MANAGEMENT
of TYPE 2
DIABETES

Javier Morales, MD
Clinical Trials Investigator
Vice President, Advanced Internal Medicine Group, PC
New Hyde Park, New York

David S. H. Bell, MB, FACE
Southside Endocrinology and Education
Birmingham, AL

Martha Mitchell Funnell, MS, RN, CDE
Research Investigator, Department of Medical Education
Co-Director, Behavioral, Clinical and Health Systems Research
Core, Michigan Diabetes Research and Training Center,
University of Michigan Medical School

Stephen Brunton, MD, FAAFP, Editor
Adjunct Clinical Professor, Department of Family Medicine
University of North Carolina, Chapel Hill, North Carolina

novo nordisk®

PROVIDED AS A SERVICE FROM NOVO NORDISK INC.

The information in this book is based on the training, personal experience and research of the authors. It is intended for educational purposes, and is not meant to diagnose, prescribe, or replace medical care. Because every person and situation is unique, the authors and publisher urge the reader to check with a qualified health care professional for appropriate diagnosis and management.

© 2011 by Primary Care Publications, Inc.

15603 McCullers Ct.
Charlotte, NC 28277 USA
www.primarycarepublications.com

ISBN: 978-0-9839596-1-8

Printed in the USA

ABOUT THE AUTHORS

Javier Morales, MD, is a Diplomate of the American Board of Internal Medicine and serves on the Board of the Patient Relations Committee at St. Francis Hospital in Roslyn, New York. Dr. Morales earned his medical degree at New Jersey Medical School in Newark, New Jersey and practices internal medicine with the Advanced Internal Medicine Group in New Hyde Park, New York. He has presented approved Continuing Medical Education programs across the United States concerning the review of the most recent clinical trials involving GLP-1 agonists and DPP-4 inhibitors. His publications have appeared in *Drugs* and *Diabetes, Obesity and Metabolism*.

David S. H. Bell, MB, FACE, is a native of Northern Ireland and graduated from Queens University Medical School. After immigrating to Canada and further training in endocrinology, two years in private practice and two years on the faculty at Temple University Medical School, Dr. Bell joined the faculty at the University of Alabama Medical School where he was a Professor of Medicine for 25 years before retirement to private practice in 2005.

Dr. Bell has published over 300 articles in referenced medical journals and four books including *Diet for Life*, the story of his own weight loss. He is also a reviewer for many general medicine and endocrine journals, has served on multiple editorial boards, and has delivered invited lectures in Italy, Ireland, Canada, Australia, New Zealand, India, Singapore, Korea, Taiwan, Malaysia, the Philippines and Puerto Rico. He has been active in many clinical interventional trials for the treatment of diabetes and its complications. In addition, his clinical abilities have been recognized by his peers with his inclusion in the "Best Doctors in America" and "America's Top Doctors," since 2001, and Best Doctors for Men in *Men's Health*, in 2007, and Best Doctors for Women in *Women's Health*, in 2008. In 2001, he was presented the Distinguished Clinician award by the American College of Endocrinology for outstanding contributions as a master educator and clinician, and, in 2002, the Seale Harris Award by the Southern Medical Association for superior contributions to the art and science of diabetes and endocrinology.

Martha Mitchell Funnell, MS, RN, CDE, is a Research Investigator in the Department of Medical Education of the University of Michigan Medical School, Co-Director of the Behavioral, Clinical and Health Systems Research Core of the MDRTC and an adjunct faculty member in the School of Nursing. She is a past President, Health Care and Education, of the American Diabetes Association, has won numerous national awards for her work, and currently is Chair of the National Diabetes Education Program. She has twenty-six years experience as a Diabetes Educator with more than 150 publications and has made over 200 presentations. Her research and publication efforts have primarily been in the field of patient empowerment and diabetes self-management education.

Stephen A. Brunton, MD, FAAFP, is a board-certified family physician, with a certificate of added qualifications in geriatrics. He holds the faculty rank of Adjunct Clinical Professor in the Department of Family Medicine at the University of North Carolina (UNC), Chapel Hill. He practices and teaches at the Cabarrus Family Medicine Residency in Harrisburg, North Carolina.

He is also Executive Director of the Primary Care Metabolic Group, an association of primary care clinicians with an interest in metabolic disease in general, and diabetes in particular.

A former president of the California Academy of Family Physicians and the Association of Family Medicine Residency Directors (AFMRD), Dr. Brunton has held many positions within the American Academy of Family Physicians (AAFP). He served as director of the division of education in the early 1980s and was a family practice residency director in California for 13 years.

A frequent lecturer, Dr. Brunton also has published numerous articles, chapters, and monographs on family medicine and related clinical topics. He serves in editorial capacities for *Clinical Diabetes, Internal Medicine Alert, Journal of Gastroenterology and Hepatology*, and *The Journal of Clinical Hypertension*. He also serves as a reviewer for *American Family Physician*, the *Southern Medical Journal*, and the *Journal of Family Practice*.

The authors would like to thank Richard Bell Smith and Elizabeth L. Smith for their assistance in developing this manuscript.

TABLE OF CONTENTS

Your doctor has given you this guide, ***The Essential Guide to the Management of Type 2 Diabetes***, because you have type 2 diabetes. Today, type 2 diabetes is so common, you probably know several other people with the disease. Your type of diabetes is found in children as well as adults. More than 20 million people in the United States have diabetes, and most of them (90-95%) have type 2 diabetes. Currently, more than a million-and-a-half new cases of diabetes are diagnosed each year in people 20 years of age and older. And, the number of people being diagnosed with diabetes is occurring at an explosive rate! As you can easily see, you are not alone!

It's only natural that you have concerns about your type 2 diabetes. This guide was written to help you to deal with some of those concerns. It will help you:

- **Better understand your diabetes;**
- **Learn some steps you can take to control your diabetes;**
- **Recognize some of the complications of diabetes;**
- **Know some of the medicines used in managing diabetes; and**
- **Assist your doctor in treating your diabetes.**

Presently, there is no known cure for diabetes. However, the good news is that your diabetes can be controlled when you work closely with your doctor and other health care professionals.

This guide is for informational purposes only. It should not replace any instructions you have received from your doctor about your type 2 diabetes. It may further explain the information and advice your health care provider has given to you. It also may be of help in answering some of the questions you have about your diabetes and the ways that you can have a favorable life style.

Be sure to talk with your doctor and follow his or her instructions about the ways to manage your diabetes. Together, you both can work out a treatment plan that should achieve the results that you desire.

Finding out that you have type 2 diabetes should not be discouraging, because you can live a long, healthy, and happy life with the disease – if you stick to your treatment plan.

– Stephen Brunton, MD, FAAFP, Editor

MANAGING YOUR DIABETES

Good self-management is the key to successfully taking care of your type 2 diabetes, and it's guided by monitoring your blood sugar levels. Comprehensive care also includes diet, exercise, medicine, and education. Your doctor will suggest any necessary testing along the line, to see how well you're managing your blood sugar and to look for any problems that may arise. You'll be pleasantly surprised at how easy it is to live with type 2 diabetes, when you learn how to manage the disease and put that learning into practice.

TYPE 2 DIABETES
CONTRIBUTING FACTORS

The factors that contribute to type 2 diabetes fall into two groups – those you can control and those over which you have no control. The leading factor for having type 2 diabetes – and one you cannot do anything about – is your family history. The chances of having diabetes is about 1 in 7 if you have a parent with type 2 diabetes, and if both your parents have it, your chance of having type 2 diabetes is almost 40%.

Race and ethnic background are other factors beyond your control. African Americans, Hispanic/Latino Americans, Native Americans, and some Asian Americans and Native Hawaiians all have a higher chance of having type 2 diabetes.

©iStockPhoto.com/Get4Net

Factors that you can control, or at least have some degree over, come under the heading of lifestyle changes. They are diet, body weight, and physical activity. Our Westernized lifestyle – too much dietary fat, too much carbohydrate (kar-boh-HY-drate), and too little fiber, in addition to not enough exercise – are environmental factors that most certainly have contributed to the rise in type 2 diabetes in the United States.

Diet

For decades, diets high in saturated fats (sat fats) and sugar and low in fiber have been linked to the development of type 2 diabetes. More recently, dietary studies have shown that vegetable oils and polyunsaturated fats (unsat fats) have a role in lowering the chance for developing type 2 diabetes. On the other hand, trans-fats, found in many fried foods, increase the chance of developing the disease.

As far as sugar is concerned, the American Diabetes Association (ADA) states that the total **amount** of sugars and starches, that is, carbohydrates (kar-boh-HY-drates) or carbs, in meals or snacks is more important than the **kinds** of carbohydrates that you eat. The ADA recommends that carbohydrates in whole-grains, fruits, vegetables, and low-fat milk be included as part of a healthy diet. There is no such thing as a "diabetic diet," and no foods are forbidden.

There are a variety of ways to plan meals that can help you manage your carbohydrates and weight. In general, spreading your carbs out over the day by eating 3 to 5 small meals will make it easier to keep your blood sugar on target. If you want a more specific plan, meeting with a dietitian is suggested. Such a meeting is often covered by insurance for people with diabetes. Before you meet with the dietitian, write down the foods you usually eat. Be sure to include those foods that are important to you and that bring you pleasure. Remember, caring for diabetes is not like being on a diet for a short time, so it is important to create a personal plan that you can use on a daily basis.

For example, you might try a divided plate approach for meals. Draw an imaginary line down the center of a plate. Fill one side with vegetables or fruit. Then, divide the remaining portion in half. Fill one section with lean meat and the last portion with starches, grains, or bread. Try to keep your portions no more than one inch high.

Divided Plate Approach

Body Weight

If you are overweight – as are most people who develop type 2 diabetes – weight loss is an important objective in controlling your disease. Even what may seem minor reductions in weight, such as 5% to 7%, can reap major benefits. Weight loss programs by themselves, however, should be combined with other lifestyle changes, particularly more physical activity, so that weight loss will be more effective in the long run.

Physical Activity

It is important to include exercise in your lifestyle changes. Exercise is very helpful in maintaining your weight loss. Additionally; exercise has been shown to reduce the risk of heart-associated risk factors, such as cardiovascular

disease, high cholesterol levels, and high blood pressure. The American Diabetes Association now recommends that people with diabetes should not go for more than two days without some form of physical activity. The good news is that you do not have to join a gym or start jogging. Activities, such as brisk walking, water aerobics, exercise videos, stationary bike or treadmill workouts at home, and dancing are all physical activities. The most important thing is to find something that you can enjoy and do regularly.

MAKING LIFESTYLE CHANGES

©iStockPhoto.com/Danny Ben-Simon

Most people find that one of the hardest things about caring for diabetes is making changes in their eating, exercise and other habits. After all, the other priorities and demands of your life do not go away when you get diabetes. It is easy to get overwhelmed and give up.

One idea that works for many people is to focus on one change at a time. Taking a big goal and breaking it down into steps helps people to be more successful and feel more confident so they can then make other changes.

For example, let's say you want to get more physical activity. Your goal is to walk 30 minutes a day 5 days a week, but you know that you will need to work up to that level. So, you decide to walk around the block after lunch 3 days this week. At the end of the week, you determine how it went. If it worked, great! You may want to add some more time or distance, or you may want to stay at this level until it becomes part of your daily routine. If your plan did not work, don't think that you've failed. Instead, figure out what went wrong and what might make the plan work better next time. Maybe having a friend or a co-worker with you would help. Keep trying until you figure out what does work for you.

Making changes takes time and effort. Take them one day and one step at a time and you will reach your goals.

YOUR EMOTIONS AND DIABETES

You can expect to have a lot of strong feelings when you find out that you have diabetes and as you continue to live with it. These feelings include denial, anger, fear, guilt, frustration, sadness and even depression. These feelings are so common that they are referred to as "diabetes-related distress." Most people find that their feelings change over time, or may not be as strong at other times, but never completely go away.

Because your emotions affect how you take care of yourself and your health, it is important to find ways to cope with diabetes-related distress. Some ideas are:

- Find a good listener. Talking about how you feel is the first step in learning to cope. If you do not have anyone to talk with, try writing your feelings down as a way to think about them.

- Join a support group for people with diabetes. Being with others who have the same struggles can help you get ideas for ways to make it easier to manage and live with diabetes. Also, being of help to others in a support group can also help you to feel better about your own situation.

- Think about how you coped with difficult things in the past. Often the same ideas will work for handling diabetes.

- Let your family and others in your life know how they can support you. For example, you might ask them to listen to you, not nag you, eat the same meals, or exercise with you.

- Practice your religion, meditate and pray. Many members of the clergy are also trained in counseling.
- Ask your doctor for a referral to a counselor. There are often free services available or services based on your ability to pay.

If you find that you are sad and depressed most of the time or your feelings are getting in the way of taking care of your diabetes, be sure to let your healthcare provider know right away. Clinical depression is a possibility among people with diabetes, but there is help available.

TYPE 2 DIABETES DEFINED

Glucose (the simplest form of sugar) is the basic fuel that all the cells in your body need. When you eat, your body breaks down different types of sugars and starches into glucose, which enters your bloodstream. Insulin is the hormone in your body that carries glucose from your bloodstream into your body cells in order to provide necessary energy for them to function properly. Insulin is produced by your pancreas (PAN-kree-us). The pancreas is a large gland, behind your stomach, that aids in digestion.

In type 2 diabetes, two things happen. Your pancreas does not produce enough insulin to do its job, and your body cells resist the entrance of sugar-carrying insulin. Because of this, you end up with too much sugar in your blood. As a result, your cells cannot function properly. And, over time, the high sugar levels in your blood may damage the nerves and blood vessels of your eyes, kidneys, brain, and

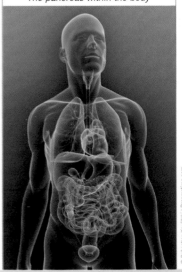

The Pancreas

The pancreas within the body

heart, or the nerves in your legs and feet.

Insulin is produced in your pancreas by beta cells. These cells make and release insulin. Beta cells help deliver insulin in the right amount at the right time, such as, when your blood sugar is too high, like after meals. Also, when you eat, there's another hormone in your body that helps your pancreas make the right amount of insulin needed to move sugar from your blood into your cells. It is called GLP-1. When your blood sugar is too high, GLP-1 stimulates the beta cells in your pancreas to produce insulin. GLP-1 also helps to lower the amount of sugar made by your liver.

With Type 2 diabetes, your beta cells quit working and start to die. As you have fewer and fewer beta cells, your pancreas makes less and less insulin. Several other things may be wrong as well:

- Your beta cells have to make more insulin than normal;
- GLP-1 does not work the way it should, so not enough insulin is made by your pancreas;
- The insulin that is made is not being used efficiently by your body cells; or
- Your liver releases too much sugar into your blood stream at the wrong times, such as when you have just eaten.

Don't be surprised if changes are made in the treatment of your type 2 diabetes from time-to-time, because it is a progressive disease. That is, it advances in severity as time passes. Over time, new treatments may be needed. You can expect your treatment plan to be changed as you continue to work to control your diabetes.

These terms seem to be a mouthful, but an easy way to think about them is to learn that "hyper" means too much, and "hypo" means too little, and that "glycemia" (gly-SEE-mee-uh) is the presence of sugar in the blood.

Hyperglycemia (HY-per-gly-SEE-mee-uh), then, is the technical term for high blood sugar, or too much sugar in the blood. When you have hyperglycemia over a long period of time, it can damage your nerves and blood vessels, and other parts of your body. Even when you think that your diabetes is under control, you can from time to time have periods of hyperglycemia, for many reasons. Some of these reasons can be the particular food you have eaten, drinking alcoholic or high-calorie beverages, situations that cause emotional upsets, illness, gaining weight, or not getting enough physical exercise.

Some of the early symptoms of hyperglycemia can be:

- **Frequent bathroom trips;**
- **Increased thirst;**
- **Blurred vision;**
- **Fatigue; or**
- **Headache**

The best way to combat hyperglycemia is to stick closely to the treatment plan that you and your doctor agree upon. When necessary, you may have to change or add medications.

Hypoglycemia (HY-po-gly-SEE-mee-uh) is the technical term for too low blood sugar. It can happen even when you're doing everything possible to control your blood sugar. It may occur when you're starting to control your blood sugar, so you should learn to recognize it – and you should let your doctor know if it happens. Your body needs a steady supply of sugar as an energy source, and if that supply is not available, some of the symptoms of hypoglycemia may occur. **These symptoms can include:**

- **Confusion;**
- **Abnormal behavior;**
- **Double or blurred vision**
- **Heart palpitations;**
- **Tremor;**
- **Anxiety;**
- **Sweating, or**
- **Hunger**

When an episode of hypoglycemia occurs, it's very often due to the medications you're taking. For this reason, you need to keep in touch with your doctor about your blood sugar levels. Again, the best way to prevent hypoglycemia is to stick closely to the treatment plan that you and your doctor have developed.

PROBLEMS SEEN WITH TYPE 2 DIABETES

Type 2 diabetes, especially if not well controlled, can lead to a number of serious health problems. Many diabetes problems don't have to happen. It's a fact that many people with type 2 diabetes never run into serious health problems caused by their disease, because they take charge of their illness and take care of themselves. Nonetheless, you should be aware of some of the problems that untreated, or poorly treated, high blood sugar can cause. The most important thing you can do to prevent these problems is to keep your blood sugar under control.

Heart Problems

One of the most severe long range problems seen in people with type 2 diabetes is heart disease. People with diabetes have a higher-than-

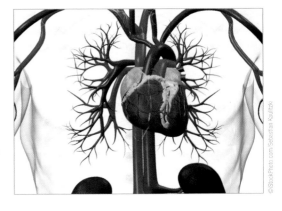

average chance of having a heart attack or a stroke. Heart disease is the leading cause of death in patients with diabetes, especially in women. Women with diabetes are 4 times more likely to have heart failure than women without the disease.

There's a lot you can do to keep your heart and blood vessels healthy. Staying with the treatment plan you and your doctor have decided upon is extremely important. Regular checkups with your doctor are also very important.

Neuropathy

Leg and foot problems are commonly seen among people with type 2 diabetes. They most often happen when you have peripheral (puh-RIF-uh-rul) neuropathy (ne-ROP-uh-thee), the medical term for nerve damage. Continued high levels of blood sugar over several years can damage the tiny blood vessels that feed your nerves. With peripheral neuropathy, you lose feeling in one or both feet or legs, and sometimes your fingers. Because of nerve damage, your ability to feel pain,

©iStockPhoto.com/Robert Kneschke

heat, and cold in your hands and feet is lessened. The loss of feeling in your feet means that you may not feel a stone or a sharp object in your shoes while walking. For this reason, if you have diabetic neuropathy, you should never walk barefoot – even indoors. People with diabetes are advised to look at the bottoms of their feet each day. Keep a small mirror handy, by your bed or in the bathroom. Use it daily to look for any damage, particularly blisters to your feet. Some people wear special shoes that help prevent their feet from getting blisters or calluses. With diabetes, you should always wear socks and dry between your toes after bathing.

There is another form of neuropathy that can occur in people with type 2 diabetes, called autonomic (aw-toh-NOM-ik) neuropathy. It affects the nerves that control the stomach, bowels, bladder, penis, and other body organs. Symptoms resulting from autonomic neuropathy can include stomach ache, diarrhea, constipation, inability to empty the bladder, and an ability to obtain and/or maintain an erection (erectile dysfunction or ED). Stomach problems, however, are more often seen in people with type 1 diabetes. Nonetheless, it's

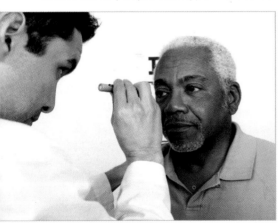

moodboard/Jupiter Images

a good idea to have a list of all your complaints and concerns with you whenever you see your doctor.

Eye Disorders

You may have heard that diabetes can lead to blindness. However, most people with diabetes do not have major sight problems and have only minor eye disorders. Too much blood sugar can damage the blood vessels in the back of the eye and lead to a condition known as retinopathy (REH-tih-NOP-uh-thee). It's possible to have retinopathy and not know it, since there usually are no symptoms of diabetic retinopathy. Retinopathy *can* lead to blindness, if high blood sugar continues over a long period of time and is not treated. Keeping your blood sugar levels under control is the best way to guard against retinopathy or, at least, reducing its severity. A yearly eye exam is very important in detecting and monitoring diabetic retinopathy. Without an annual eye exam, retinopathy will not be diagnosed and, therefore, cannot be treated to prevent or limit its damage.

Skin Disorders

Nearly one-third of people with diabetes will have a diabetes related skin disorder at some time in their lives. Skin disorders are many times the first sign that a person has diabetes. Most anyone can have some of these skin disorders, such as bacterial infections, fungal infections, and itching. Several kinds of bacterial infections can occur in people with diabetes:

- Infections of the glands of the eyelids;
- Boils;
- Infections of the hair roots;
- Carbuncles (deep infections of the skin and tissue underneath); and
- Infections around the fingernails or toenails.

Yeast or fungal infections occur more frequently in people with diabetes, especially when sugar levels are continually high. These usually occur in the warm, moist folds of the skin. The most common ones:

- Athlete's foot;
- Jock itch;

- Ringworm; and

- Vaginal infections.

Local areas of itching are often caused by diabetes. They can be caused by a yeast infection, dry skin, or poor circulation. When poor circulation is the cause of itching, the areas most affected are the lower parts of the leg.

Hearing Disorders

According to the National Institutes of Health (NIH), hearing loss is twice as common in people with diabetes as it is among those who don't have the disease. Hearing depends upon the correct functioning of small blood vessels 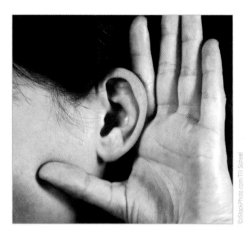 and nerves in the inner ear. High blood sugar levels can damage these vessels and nerves, and, over time, the ability to hear is reduced. Often, family members or friends notice hearing loss before the person with such loss realizes it.

High Blood Pressure

As many as 2 out of 3 adults with diabetes have high blood pressure, or hypertension (HY-per-TEN-shun). The combination of high blood pressure and diabetes increases your risk of eye disease, heart attack, kidney disease, and stroke. People with diabetes

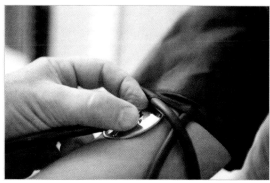
©iStockPhoto.com/webphotographeer

have a lower blood pressure goal than those without the disease. Both the American Diabetes Association and the National Institutes of Health recommend that people with diabetes should have a blood pressure of one-thirty over eighty (130/80 mmHg) or below. Treatment for high blood pressure differs from one person to the next. However, both lifestyle changes, particularly weight loss and restricted salt and alcohol intake, and medicines can help you keep your blood pressure under control.

Stroke

A stroke happens when the blood supply to part of your brain is blocked or a blood vessel ruptures and brain tissue is damaged. A blocked blood vessel is the most common cause of a stroke. A stroke can cause paralysis, problems with thinking or speaking, and emotional problems.

If you have diabetes, you're much more likely to have heart disease, a heart attack, or a stroke. While just having diabetes puts you at risk for these conditions, your risk is even greater under the following conditions:

- High cholesterol levels;
- Family history of strokes or TIAs (transient ischemic attacks), also called mini-strokes;
- High blood pressure; and
- Cigarette smoking

©iStockPhoto.com/Steve Cole

Avoiding Problems

The list of possible problems that can arise when you have type 2 diabetes is a long one. Happily, working with your health care team, there are many steps that you can take to avoid these problems. The most important one is controlling your blood sugar. And, if any of these health problems occur, prompt treatment can either resolve them or lessen their effects. The good news is that scientific knowledge and modern medicine have come a long way forward in the diagnosis, treatment, and management of type 2 diabetes. You have a much greater chance than your parents or grandparents had of leading a long and happy life with the disease.

Diabetes can be especially difficult in women. Many women who are diagnosed with type 2 diabetes already have heart disease. Many women have risk factors of heart disease, such as high cholesterol levels, high blood pressure, or stomach obesity.

Pregnancy

Gestational (jes-TAY-shun-ul) diabetes develops during pregnancy in 2 to 5 percent of pregnant women and disappears when the pregnancy is over.

However, women who have had gestational diabetes or those who have delivered a baby weighing more than 9 pounds are at an increased risk of developing type 2 diabetes later in life.

Women with type 2 diabetes are able to have healthy babies. If you're in that group, you too, can have healthy babies with strict diabetes control and close medical supervision of your pregnancy. If you have type 2 diabetes and are taking pills to control your disease, you will most likely have to switch to insulin when you get pregnant.

Depression

Major depression is tied up with a combination of symptoms that interfere with the ability to work, study, sleep, eat, and enjoy activities that were once fun. Depression is seen much more often in people with type 2 diabetes than in those without the disease. Women also are twice as likely as men to have depression, and it is believed that female hormones play a role in this increased rate of depression. Many women also face unique stresses that can lead to depression –

©iStockPhoto.com/Eduardo Jose Bernardino

responsibilities both at work and at home, single parenthood, and caring for children and aging parents.

Eating Disorders

Eating disorders are illnesses. They are affected by emotional and cultural factors. Our American society has attached a mark of shame to eating disorders. As a result, many women suffer in silence. Both society and many medical professionals have failed to recognize the dangerous consequences of eating disorders, particularly when they affect women with type 2 diabetes.

There has been some amount of media attention paid to eating disorders, particularly among famous people in the tabloids. They can also occur in men but are much more common in women.

The most common disorders are:

- **Anorexia** (an-or-EX-ee-uh): Self-starvation and excessive weight loss;

- **Bulimia** (boo-LEE-me-uh): Rapid excessive eating, followed by getting rid of the food by vomiting, using laxatives, or fasting;

- **Binge eating:** Continuous eating beyond the point of feeling full; and

- **Too much exercise** leading to excessive weight loss.

Help is available for all these eating disorders, and full recovery is to be expected with this help.

Sexual Concerns

Diabetes can affect a woman's sex life. Some women with type 2 diabetes are affected by vaginal dryness at an earlier age than normal, which can make sexual intercourse painful. This problem of vaginal dryness may be traced to damaged nerves that normally would help provide lubrication. Medicines that can help with the dryness are available.

MEN WITH TYPE 2 DIABETES

Diabetes can affect a man's sex life, also. Historically, men have been unwilling to talk about their health, including diabetes, and especially about any sexual problems they might have. Times have changed, however, and men today are much more open about their diseases and the problems they present. Men with diabetes often have erectile dysfunction, commonly called ED. Erectile dysfunction can prevent a man from having or keeping an erection. This condition usually results from damaged nerves that supply the blood vessels in the penis. The damage can come from too much sugar in the bloodstream.

ED can be caused by a number of other conditions. Medicines for high blood pressure, depression, stomach ulcers, or heartburn can cause ED. Prostate or bladder surgery may result in ED. Low testosterone (tess-TAHS-tear-own) levels can also cause ED. Testosterone is a body hormone that causes the male sex organs to function. Men with type 2 diabetes are twice as likely to have low testosterone levels as men without the disease.

If you're suffering from ED, it's important to work with your doctor to find the cause. Today, there are a number of medications to treat ED, and even more are on the way.

DIABETES AND CARDIOVASCULAR DISEASE

Cardiovascular (car-dee-oh-VAS-cue-lar) disease is a general term that groups all of the diseases of the heart and blood vessels. The American Heart Association considers diabetes as 1 of 6 risk factors for cardiovascular disease that can be controlled. Adults with diabetes are 2 to 4 times more likely to have heart disease or stroke than adults of the same age that do not have diabetes. People with type 2 diabetes often have several conditions that increase their risk for cardiovascular disease. Most of these have been pointed out earlier in this guide. They are high blood pressure, obesity, lack of physical activity, poorly-controlled blood sugar, and cigarette smoking.

An important cardiovascular risk factor that you can control is a cholesterol (koh-LES-ter-all) level that is not normal. Cholesterol in itself isn't all bad – a certain amount is needed to keep your body functioning properly. Cholesterol is a fat-like substance that travels around your body as a fat, or lipid (LIP-id) attached to a protein. Thus, it is named a lipoprotein (lie-poe-PRO-teen).

There are two kinds of cholesterol – HDL (high-density lipoprotein) and LDL (low-density lipoprotein). HDL is known as good cholesterol, because it carries "leftover" cholesterol away from your arteries and back to your liver, where it is passed from your body. High levels of HDL appear to protect against a heart attack. Unfortunately, in type 2 diabetes, the levels tend to be lower and the HDL particles smaller, which reduces the effect of carrying any leftover cholesterol to your liver.

LDL is also known as bad cholesterol, because too much of it can build up in the walls of your arteries that supply blood to your heart and your brain. This buildup is called plaque. Plaque causes the arteries to narrow and make them less flexible. If a clot forms where there is a narrowing of the artery and blocks one of these narrowed arteries, a heart attack or stroke can follow.

People with diabetes may have normal total and LDL cholesterol levels, but the LDL particles may be smaller and denser and more easily stick to their arteries where they form plaques. For this reason, doctors recommend lower LDL levels for people with diabetes.

Your doctor can order a simple blood test that will measure your cholesterol levels. If your levels are not normal, the two of you can work out a plan for dealing with whatever lifestyle changes or medicines will be needed to correct them.

Your treatment plan, in addition to lifestyle changes and medications, will require several kinds of tests. Also, your doctor will prescribe any needed medicines. Self-treatment, however, is the cornerstone of managing your diabetes. It will largely be up to you to follow the treatment plan.

Numbers to Know

To stay on top of your disease, you're going to have to learn some numbers. Three essential numbers are known as the ABCs of diabetes.

- "A" stands for A1C (A-one-C). It is a blood test that measures your average blood sugar level over the last three months. The test measures the percentage of your red blood cells that are coated with sugar. The ideal percentage is 7 or less. To achieve this number, you'll most likely need to combine diet, exercise, and medicine. However, if hypoglycemia becomes a problem, levels of above 7 may be acceptable, but this situation needs to be discussed with your doctor.

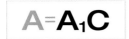

$$A = A_1C$$

- "B" is for blood pressure. Your blood pressure target is 130/80 or below. It should be taken each time you visit your doctor. A target level of 120/70 or below may be needed if you also have kidney disease. You can also measure your blood pressure at home using a meter and a cuff. Relax first, and don't cross your legs as the cuff deflates.

- "C" means cholesterol. Your target should be an LDL level below 100 and an HDL level above 40 in a man, and above 50 in a woman. Again, diet and exercise can help, and there are also medicines your doctor may want you to use to achieve these numbers.

To recap, the essential numbers to remember are:

- **A=7 or lower;**
- **B=130/80 or lower; and**
- **C=100 or lower for LDL, and 40-50 or higher for HDL**

Blood Sugar Testing

Checking your blood sugar yourself is often the best way to find out if your diabetes is under control. You may have to check your blood sugar daily or even several times a day. Testing involves a meter, test strips, and a lancing device. The spring-loaded lancing device holds the lancets that prick your skin. Your doctor can suggest the best test kit for you. The lancing device is used to enable you to draw a little amount of blood from one of your fingertips or forearms. You'll apply the small amount of blood to your meter's test strip.

Some of the more recent blood sugar test kits permit you to draw blood from other parts of your body, such as your arms. Pin-pricks in the forearm, upper arm, thigh, or calf

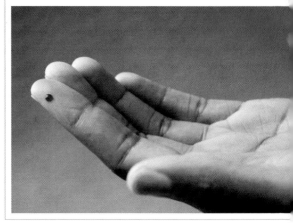

A small sample of blood for glucose testing

are less painful than those in the fingers. Fingerstick readings tell you your blood sugar level at the moment you take them. However, readings from other parts of your body can be up to 30 minutes old. If you were to have a rapid fall in blood sugar and experience symptoms of hypoglycemia, the situation might not be immediately detected using pin-pricks from other parts of your body

The target values for blood sugar tests are between 70 and 130 before meals and less than 180 two hours after meals.

To test your blood sugar, follow the instructions that come with your test kit. There are five simple steps usually involved in blood sugar testing.

©iStockPhoto.com/Mark Hatfield

In the early stages of type 2 diabetes, in addition to diet and exercise to help control your disease, you will probably have to rely on one or more oral medicines (medicines that you take by mouth). Diabetes pills work best when you also follow a meal plan and get regular physical activity. There are many types of diabetes pills. They work in different ways to lower blood sugar levels.

- **Some pills help the body release more insulin.** They help the beta cells in the pancreas release insulin, resulting in a lowering of blood sugar. This helps keep blood sugar levels in the target range. Some of these medicines are known as meglitinides (meg-LIT-in-ides). They leave the bloodstream quickly so insulin levels return to baseline between meals and during the night. Other medicines called sulfonylureas (SULL-fon-ill-you-REE-uz) work up to 24 hours. If you take these types of pills, be sure to eat regularly.

- **Some pills reduce the amount of sugar the liver releases.** These medicines are classified as biguanides (bye-GWAN-ides). They help improve the body's ability to use insulin. They are usually taken twice a day with food.

- **Some pills help insulin work better in muscle and fat.** Insulin resistance can be a problem for many people with type 2 diabetes. Insulin resistance is what happens when the cells and tissues in the body can't use insulin properly. Some medicines called thiazolidinediones (thigh-uh-ZOLL-ih-dean-DIE-owns) help insulin work better in muscle and fat. They make the body respond to the insulin that it already makes. This means that more sugar leaves the blood. The sugar enters the muscles and the fat cells, where it belongs. This helps lower blood sugar levels. These medicines are taken once or twice a day.

- **Some medicines slow the breakdown of food into sugar.** These medicines are called alpha glucosidase (owl-fuh-glue-CO-sid-ace) inhibitors. They help keep blood sugar from rising too high after a meal. They are taken at the start of a meal.

Depending on your treatment needs, you may need to take more than one of these medicines to control your diabetes as it progresses. The action of the different types of medicines can complement one another and help to lower your blood sugar levels.

Diabetes medicines that are taken by mouth do not work for everyone. Sometimes they do not bring blood sugar levels down low enough… or they stop working after a few months or years. This may happen because of the loss of beta cell function over time for people with type 2 diabetes. This does not mean that you have failed to control your diabetes. It simply means that your body has changed and needs a different type of treatment.

INCRETINS AND NEWER MEDICINES FOR TYPE 2 DIABETES

The newest class of medicines for type 2 diabetes is known as incretin-based (in-KRET-in) medications. They take their name from hormones in your gut that increase insulin secretion, called incretins. GLP-1 is an incretin that your body naturally produces when you eat. GLP-1 signals the beta cells in your pancreas to make insulin when your body needs it. Your liver stores extra sugar from the foods you eat and releases it when you need it. GLP-1 also helps stop your liver from releasing sugar that you do not need. Incretin-based agents improve beta cell function, stimulate insulin secretion, and reduce appetite. They are divided into two groups – GLP-1 agonists and DPP-4 inhibitors.

GLP-1 Medicines

GLP-1 medicines are non-insulin injectable medicines. They may be taken once or twice a day, depending on the medicine. These non-insulin injectable medicines work in one or more of the following ways:

- By acting like a hormone called GLP-1. This helps manage blood sugar by helping beta cells release more insulin when blood sugar is too high;

- By stopping the liver from releasing sugar into the blood when it is not needed; or

- By slowing the movement of food through the stomach so sugar enters the blood more slowly.

DPP-4 Inhibitor Medicines

DPP-4 inhibitor medicines work to block an enzyme in your body called DPP-4. The DPP-4 in your body breaks down your body's own GLP-1. So when DPP-4 is blocked, your GLP-1 levels rise. Like the GLP-1 medicines, DPP-4 medicines improve beta cell function and stimulate the release of insulin. However, there are some notable differences in the ways these medicines are seen to act. DPP-4 medicines have a smaller effect on the rise in overnight blood sugar levels, and they have a smaller effect on appetite. DPP-4 medicines are in the form of tablets.

Reference Chart for Type 2 Diabetes Medicine

Type of Medicine	Route
Meglitinides	Oral
Sulfonylureas	Oral
Biguanides	Oral
Thiazolidinediones	Oral
Alpha-Glucosidase Inhibitors	Oral
GLP-1 agonists	Injectable
DPP-4 Inhibitors	Oral

How They Work	Dosing Schedule
Help beta cells release insulin	1-4 times daily
Help beta cells release insulin	1 or 2 times daily
Lower sugar production by the liver	1 or 2 times daily
Help cells and tissues use insulin	1 or 2 times daily
Slow digestion of sugar	Before each meal
Help beta cells release insulin, stop release of un-needed sugar by liver, slow emptying of the stomach	Inject once or twice daily
Help beta cells release insulin and decrease glucagon secretion	Once daily

USING INSULIN TO CONTROL YOUR TYPE 2 DIABETES

As you've learned, type 2 diabetes is a progressive disease. You'll probably have to change or add to your medicines as time goes by. Someday, it is probable that your pancreas will not be able to supply the amount of insulin your body will need. If that happens, you'll need to get insulin from an outside source. This happens to about 40% of people with type 2 diabetes and usually can occur within ten years after the disease is diagnosed.

Insulin, today, is a far cry from what your grandma used! Not only are there new kinds of insulin, but there are more convenient and painless ways to inject them.

Insulins vary according to how long before they start and continue to work in your body. Your doctor will determine the type and amount of insulin you need in order to achieve your best blood sugar levels.

Insulin has to be injected, because stomach acid destroys it, so that pills and capsules cannot be used. However, newer, thinner, shorter needles make such an injection almost pain-less. And, there are also injection devices (pens) that make it easy and convenient to set in advance the amount of insulin your body needs.

Needle phobia (fear) used to be a real issue when it came to self-administered insulin injections. No one enjoys being stuck with a needle. A person may have bad recollections of having injections, stemming from childhood experiences ("This isn't going to hurt"— but it does!), or in the military, many shots given all at once leaving you with a sore arm for several days.

Today's types of insulin and their delivery systems are a far cry from those of the past. Needles are thinner and shorter, and you can barely feel the needle as it enters your skin. In many cases, you don't feel the needle prick at all.

Types of Insulin

Insulin comes in several different forms. Each kind of insulin works at a different speed and lasts for a different length of time.

How to Take Insulin

Insulin Pen Method

Insulin pens come in two basic styles: disposable and reusable. Disposable pens are prefilled with insulin, stored in the refrigerator until opened, and, once opened, are stored at room temperature. When the insulin is used up, the pens are thrown away. Reusable pens are loaded with separately purchased insulin cartridges. The cartridges of insulin are stored in the refrigerator until placed in the pen, but the reusable pen is not refrigerated.

With both types of pens, you screw on a special needle that is thrown away after each use. You dial in a dose, insert the needle into your skin, and press a button to inject the insulin.

Insulin Pen

Vial and Syringe Method

There are some basic steps involved in giving yourself insulin.

1. Wash your hands.

2. Wipe the top of the insulin bottle with an alcohol swab. Also wipe the area of skin where you intend to inject your insulin with an alcohol swab.

3. Remove the needle cover of the syringe. Pull back the plunger of the syringe until it shows the dose you need.

4. Insert the syringe needle into the top of the insulin bottle and push the plunger forward. Turn the bottle and the syringe upside down.

5. Pull back on the syringe plunger until it draws the amount of insulin you need into the syringe.

6. Remove the filled syringe from the bottle. Holding the syringe at a 90-degree angle, insert the needle all the way into your skin and push the plunger forward. If you're thin, it's sometimes easier to inject the insulin at a 45-degree angle.

7. Remove the syringe and dispose of it in the way your doctor recommends.

CONCLUSIONS

The four, most important things you must know about managing your type 2 diabetes are:

1. Recognize that there is no cure;

2. Your disease will last a lifetime;

3. Your treatment will change over time, either when it no longer works or when new products to control blood sugar that will help in your particular case are brought on the market; and

4. You must stick to your treatment program to live a long, happy and productive life.

It can't be said too often, and it bears repeating here. *Good self-management is the key to successfully taking care of your type 2 diabetes, and it's guided by monitoring your blood sugar levels. Comprehensive care also includes diet,*

exercise, medicine, and education. Your doctor will suggest any necessary testing along the line, to see how well you're managing your blood sugar and to look for any problems that may arise. You'll be pleasantly surprised at how easy it is to live with type 2 diabetes, when you learn how to manage the disease and put that learning into practice.

©iStockPhoto.com/Kuzma

Diabetes Support Groups

All across the United States there are diabetes support groups that can help you manage your diabetes. Most are located in local hospitals, and many can be found in community centers.

Patient Education Websites

- American Diabetes Association: http://www.diabetes.org or http://www.diabetes.org/espanol (in Spanish)
- National Institutes of Health: http://vsearch.nlm.nih.gov/vivisimo/cgi-bin/query-meta?v%3A project=medlineplus&query=diabetes&x=9&y=13
- American Academy of Family Physicians. Living with Diabetes: http://content.yudu.com/A1gpo2/LivingWithDiabetes/ resources/index.htm
- AAFP Patient Education Resource: http://familydoctor.org
- Diabetes Medicines: http://www.cornerstones4care.com
- Changing Diabetes: http://www.ChangingDiabetes-us.com
- Type 2 diabetes information: http://www.diabetes.com
- Type 2 diabetes: http://www.mayoclinic.com/health/type-2-diabetes/DS00585
- Type 2 diabetes: http://www.WhyInsulin.com

Books on Type 2 Diabetes

- Weiss MA, Funnell MM. *The Little Diabetes Book You Need to Read.* Philadelphia, PA: Running Press; 2007

GLOSSARY

A1C: Blood test that measures your average blood sugar over last 3 months.

Agonist: Medication that starts the activity of a cell.

Anorexia: Self-starvation and excessive weight loss.

Binge eating: Continuous eating beyond the point of feeling full.

Boil: Infection that causes a swelling of the skin, with a hard core and pus.

Bulimia: Rapid excessive eating, followed by getting rid of food by vomiting or using laxatives.

Callus: Thickening of skin caused by irritation.

Carbohydrate: Sugars and starches in foods.

Carbs: Nickname for carbohydrates.

Carbuncle: Deep infection of skin and tissue underneath.

Cardiovascular: Relating to the heart and blood vessels.

Cholesterol: Chemical found in foods high in animal fat.

DPP-4: Enzyme in the body that breaks down GLP-1.

ED: Nickname for erectile dysfunction.

Endocrine gland: A gland that releases hormones into the bloodstream.

Enzyme: Substance that causes chemical changes in other substances without changing its own makeup.

Erectile dysfunction: Inability by a male to have and/or maintain an erection, also known as ED.

FDA: Food and Drug Administration.

Fungal infection: Infection caused by a yeast or a mold.

Gastrointestinal: Relating to the stomach and intestines (gut).

Gestational: Occurring during pregnancy.

GLP-1: Hormone in your body that signals beta cells to release insulin and helps stop your liver from releasing sugar.

Glucagon: Hormone in the pancreas that increases the release of sugar into the bloodstream.

Glucose: Simplest form of sugar, used in the body to provide energy to the cells.

HDL: High-density lipoprotein; good cholesterol that carries leftover cholesterol from arteries to liver where it passes from the body.

Heart attack: Event that interrupts the blood supply to heart muscle.

Hemoglobin: Part of the red blood cell that carries oxygen from lungs to tissues.

Hormone: Substance from one part of the body that is carried by the blood to another part of the body where it produces its effect.

Hyperglycemia: Too much sugar in the blood.

Hypertension: High blood pressure.

Hypoglycemia: Too little sugar in the blood.

Incretins: Gastrointestinal hormones that increase insulin release from the pancreas.

Inhibitor: Medication that stops the activity of a cell.

Insulin: Hormone that causes sugar to move from the bloodstream into body cells.

Lancet: Sharp-pointed instrument that makes a small opening in the skin.

LDL: Low-density lipoprotein; bad cholesterol that forms plaque in arteries and causes them to narrow.

Lipoprotein: Lipid (fat) attached to a protein. Cholesterol is carried by lipoproteins in the blood.

Medication: Medicine.

Obesity: Excessive body fat.

Palpitation: Throbbing heartbeat.

Pancreas: Body gland that aids in digestion and releases insulin.

Pancreatitis: Inflamed pancreas.

Paralysis: Loss of motion or sensation in a part of the body.

Phobia: Dread or fear that causes panic.

Plaque: Buildup of cholesterol in arteries.

Polyunsaturated fats: Food fats that play a role in lowering the chance for developing type 2 diabetes.

Prostate: Male gland located at the base of the urethra (urinary tube).

Proteins: Large molecules that contain many of the chemicals essential for life functions.

Stroke: Loss of blood supply to the brain due to a blocked blood vessel.

Testosterone: Body hormone with several functions, particularly causing male sex organs to function.

TIA: Transient ischemic attack, or mini-stroke.

Trans-fats: Fats in many fried foods that raise the chance of developing diabetes and other cardiovascular diseases.

Unsat fats: See polyunsaturated fats.

Vaginal: Relating to the vagina, the canal that extends inward to the uterus.

QUESTIONS FOR MY DOCTOR

Write them here...

National Diabetes Statistics, 2007. Available at: http://www.diabetes.niddk.nih.gov/dm/pubs/statistics/. Accessed October 21, 2010.

Cheng D. Prevalence, predisposition and prevention of type II diabetes. *Nutr Metab (Lond)* 2005;2:29

American Diabetes Association. Genetics of Diabetes. Available at: http://www.diabetes.org/diabetes-basics/genetics-of-diabetes.html. Accessed March 8, 2011.

Powers AC. Diabetes Mellitus. In: *Harrison's Principles of Internal Medicine.* 16th ed. New York, NY: McGraw-Hill: 2005: 2152-2180.

Bazzano LA, Serdula M, Liu S. Prevention of type 2 diabetes by diet and lifestyle modification. *J AM Coll Nutr.* 2005;24:210-319.

Franz MJ, Bantle JP, Beebe CA, etal. Evidence-based nutrition principles and recommendations for the treatment and prevention of diabetes and related complications. *Diabetes Care.* 2003;26 (suppl 1):S51-S61.

Sigal RJ, Kenny GP, Wasserman DH, Castaneda-Sceppa C, White RD. Physical activity/exercise and type 2 diabetes: a consensus statement from the American Diabetes Association. *Diabetes Care.* 2006;29:1433-1438.

Skovlund SE, Peyrot M. The diabetes attitudes, wishes, and needs (DAWN) program: A new approach to improving outcomes of diabetes care. *Diabetes Spectrum.* 2005;18:136-142

American Diabetes Association. Type 2. Available at: http://www.diabetes.org/diabetes-basics/type-2/. Accessed October 25, 2010.

Diabetes and You. Changing Life with Diabetes series. 135625R2. Novo Nordisk Inc. Pages 6 &11. September 2009.

The Role of GLP-1 in the Treatment of Type 2 Diabetes. Available at: http:// www.lilly.com/pdf/GLP_Backgrounder.pdf. Accessed May 9, 2011.

Hyperglycemia in diabetes. Available at: http://www.mayoclinic.com/health/hyperglycemia/DS01168. Accessed October 28, 2010.

Hypoglycemia. Available at: http://www.mayoclinic.com/health/hypoglycemia/DS00198. Accessed October 28, 2010.

American Diabetes Association. Heart Disease. Available at: http://www.diabetes.org/living-with-diabetes/complications/heart-disease.html. Accessed October 25, 2010.

American Diabetes Association. Coronary Heart Disease. Available at: http://www.diabetes.org/living-with-diabetes/complications/women/coronary-heart-disease.html. Accessed November 2, 2010.

American Diabetes Association. Foot Complications. Available at: http://www.diabetes.org/living-with-diabetes/complications/foot-complications.html. Accessed October 25, 2010.

American Diabetes Association. Autonomic Neuropathy. Available at: http://www.diabetes.org/living-with-diabetes/complications/neuropathy/autonomic-neuropathy.html. Accessed November 3, 2010.

American Diabetes Association. Eye Complications. Available at: http://www.diabetes.org/living-with-diabetes/complications/eye-complications.html. Accessed October 25, 2010.

Diabetic retinopathy. Available at: http://www.mayoclinic.com/health/diabetic-retinopathy/DS00447. Accessed November 3, 2010.

American Diabetes Association. Skin Complications. Available at: http://www.diabetes.org/living-with-diabetes/complications/skin-complications.html. Accessed October 25, 2010.

American Diabetes Association. Diabetes and Hearing Loss. Available at: http://www.diabetes.org/living-with-diabetes/seniors/hearing-loss.html. Accessed October 25, 2010.

American Diabetes Association. High Blood Pressure (Hypertension). Available at: http://www.diabetes.org/living-with-diabetes/complications/high-blood-pressure-hypertension.html. Accessed October 25, 2010.

American Diabetes Association. Stroke. Available at: http://www.diabetes.org/living-with-diabetes/complications/stroke.html. Accessed October 25, 2010.

American Diabetes Association. Women. Available at: http://www.diabetes.org/living-with-diabetes/complications/women.html. Accessed October 25, 2010.

American Diabetes Association. Depression. Available at: http://www.diabetes.org/living-with-diabetes/complications/women/depression.html. Accessed October 25, 2010.

American Diabetes Association. Eating Disorders. Available at: http://www.diabetes.org/living-with-diabetes/complications/women/eating-disorders.html. Accessed October 25, 2010.

American Diabetes Association. Sexual Health. Available at: http://www.diabetes.org/living-with-diabetes/complications/women/sexual-health.html. Accessed October 25, 2010.

American Diabetes Association. Men's Health. Available at: http://www.diabetes.org/living-with-diabetes/complications/women/mens-health.html. Accessed October 25, 2010.

American Diabetes Association. Erectile Dysfunction. Available at: http://www.diabetes.org/living-with-diabetes/complications/mens-health/sexual-health/erectile-dysfunction.html. Accessed October 25, 2010.

American Diabetes Association. Low Testosterone. Available at: http://www.diabetes.org/living-with-diabetes/complications/mens-health/sexual-health/low-testosterone.html. Accessed October 25, 2010.

Cardiovascular Disease & Diabetes. Available at: http://www.heart.org/HEARTORG/Conditions/Diabetes/WhyDiabetesMatters/Cardiovascular/. Accessed November 4, 2010.

Good vs. Bad Cholesterol. Available at: http://www.heart.org/HEARTORG/Conditions/Cholesterol/AboutCholesterol/Good-vs-Bad-Cholesterol/. Accessed November 4, 2010.

Vijayaraghavan K. Treatment of dyslipidemia in patients with type 2 diabetes. *Lipids in Health and Disease.* 2010; 9:144-155.

A1C Test. Available at: http://www.mayoclinic.com/health/a1c-test/MY00142. Accessed November 5, 2010.

American Diabetes Association. Checking your blood glucose. Available at: http://www.diabetes.org/living-with-diabetes/treatment-and-care/blood-glucose-control/. Accessed November 5, 2010.

Diabetes treatment: Medications for type 2 diabetes. Available at: http://www.mayoclinic.com/health/diabetes-treatment/DA00089. Accessed February 16, 2011.

Diabetes Pills (OADs). Available at: http://www.diabetes.org/living-with-diabetes/treatment-and-care/medication/oral-medications/can-diabetes-pills-help-me.html Accessed August 17, 2011

Garber AJ. Incretin-based therapies in the management of type 2 diabetes: rationale and reality in a managed care setting. *Am J Manag Care.* 2010;16(Suppl):S187-S194.

Non-insulin Injectable Medicines. Available at: http://www.diabetes.org/living-with-diabetes/treatment-and-care/medication/other-injectable-medication.html Accessed August 17, 2011.

Diabetes: How to Use Insulin. Available at: http://aafp.org/990800/990800i.html. Accessed November 11, 2010.

Insulin Pens. Available at: http://forecast.diabetes.org/print/node/1861. Accessed November 12, 2010.

This amazingly comprehensive book will support people with type 2 diabetes to be successful in the care and management of their disease. It provides a learning opportunity on every page covering topics that are important and useful.

— **Davida F. Kruger, MSN, APN-BC, BC-ADM**
Certified Nurse Practitioner- Diabetes,
Henry Ford Health System, Division of Endocrinology,
Diabetes, Bone and Mineral Disease
Detroit, MI

This expertly written, yet easily understood manuscript is a must read for all patients with type 2 diabetes. Its simple format bridges the educational gaps between physician recommendations, diabetic educators, dietitians, pharmacists and patient's concerns. It answers all the questions. This could easily become "the patient handbook" for type 2 diabetes.

— **James R. LaSalle, D.O.,FAAFP**
Medical Director, Medical Arts Centers

The guide provides an excellent overview of key diabetes concepts. It's a great resource for diabetic patients and their families who wish to take control of this chronic disease.

— **Doron Schneider, MD FACP**, Medical Director,
Center for Patient Safety and Healthcare Quality, Abington
Memorial Hospital, Abington PA, Assistant Clinical Professor
of Medicine, Drexel University School of Medicine

The information in this book will empower you to improve your self-management skills to better manage your diabetes and lead a healthy life.

— **Joe Largay, PAC, CDE**
Clinical Instructor, School of Medicine
UNC Diabetes Care Center